VANISHED ON A SPRING AFTERNOON

The Lyon Sisters, a Chilling Unsolved Mystery, and the True Crime Case That Haunts America

Richie J. Garst

**Copyright © 2025 by Richie J. Garst.
All rights reserved.**

No part of this book may be copied, stored, or transmitted in any form or by any means, electronic or mechanical, including photocopying and recording, without prior written permission from the author, except for brief quotations in reviews or critical articles.

This book is a work of nonfiction. Some names and identifying details may have been changed to protect the privacy of individuals.

DISCLAIMER

This book is a work of nonfiction based on real events. Every effort has been made to present information accurately and fairly, drawing from publicly available sources, historical records, and documented accounts.

The author does not claim to provide new evidence or investigative findings. While care has been taken to ensure accuracy, some details may be subject to differing interpretations. Names, identifying details, or minor circumstances may have been changed to protect the privacy of individuals.

This book is intended for informational and educational purposes only. It is not meant to sensationalize tragedy, interfere with ongoing investigations, or cause harm to victims, their families, or communities. The author and publisher disclaim any liability for how the information is used or interpreted by readers.

CONTENTS

PROLOGUE 6
    The Deserted Street 6

CHAPTER 1 12
    Wheaton Plaza 12

CHAPTER 2 17
    Vanishing Point 17

CHAPTER 3 22
    The Hunt Begins 22

CHAPTER 4 27
    Suspicions and Leads 27

CHAPTER 5 32
    The Case Grows Cold 32

CHAPTER 6 37
    A Break in Time 37

CHAPTER 7 43
    Into Darkness 43

CHAPTER 8 49
    Justice on Trial 49

CHAPTER 9 .... **54**
    The Echoes Remain 54
EPILOGUE **59**
    Ghosts of Wheaton Plaza 59
CLOSING SECTION **62**
    Lessons from the Shadows 62
        Key Lessons Learned 62
        Modern Safety Strategies 64
        Inside the Criminal Mind 66
        Honoring the Victims 67
        Extended Resources 68

Author's Note

This book was never meant to sensationalize, but to remember. Sheila and Katherine Lyon were not just names in a case file—they were daughters, sisters, and children who deserved to grow up.

Their story reminds us how fragile innocence can be, and how vital it is to remain vigilant as communities and as individuals. It also shows us the power of persistence—that even decades later, truth can emerge.

I offer this work in honor of the Lyon sisters, and in recognition of every family who has endured the unthinkable. May their memory never fade.

PROLOGUE

The Deserted Street

It was expected that the first day of spring in 1975 would be a typical one.

The mild March briskness that clung to clothes in the morning but promised afternoon warmth was in the air in Wheaton, Maryland. At that time, Wheaton Plaza was a bustling suburban mall, and the trees that lined the walkways gave the impression that blooms were on the way. Children playing on early spring vacation added to the bustle.

The Lyon sisters, Sheila and Katherine, saw it as a little adventure. The two sisters, aged ten and twelve, were overjoyed to go to the plaza, which was just a short walk away, after lunch. By dinnertime, they said they would be returning. Their parents, concerned but trusting, permitted them to leave. It was a different period, a time when children rode bikes at sunset, when streets seemed secure, and when the concept of evil lurking close seemed almost unimaginable.

Neighbors recalled the girls as inseparable. Katherine, the younger, bright-eyed, and full of joy, trailed after her elder sister, who bore the calm responsibility of the oldest. Sheila had her father's watchful look and her mother's soft caution but yet maintained the carefree rhythm of youth. Together, they went down the sidewalk toward Wheaton Plaza, not understanding that every stride was bringing them closer to an event that would haunt their neighborhood for decades.

The square . Witnesses would subsequently report the sisters visiting the record store, pausing by the Easter display, and chatting to other youngsters near the shopping complex. Some reported they spotted the girls with a guy holding a recording recorder. Others claimed they observed nothing strange at all. Memory blurred against panic, leaving investigators with bits of a chronology that never entirely aligned.

Then—silence.

Somewhere between the record store and the open plaza, the females disappeared. No scream was heard. No one phoned for aid. They just melted into the hubbub of an average day.

One witness, years later, tried to put it into words:

> "It was like they were just gone. One moment they were there, and the next, no one could explain where they'd gone. Children don't simply disappear like that."

But they did. And that stillness would become greater with every passing hour.

By dusk, the Lyon house was fraught with uneasiness. The girls had promised to come back for supper, and the dining table remained disturbingly silent. Their father, John Lyon, paced the floor, while their mother, Mary, examined the street again and again. At first, there was denial—a feeling that the girls had lost count of time, that they would be racing through the door any moment.

But as darkness fell, terror took its place.

John Lyon's voice shattered the silence:

> "They should've been here hours ago."

Mary responded gently, attempting to settle her own panic.

> "Maybe they're still with friends. Maybe…"

But even she realized the words were empty.

Neighbors joined the hunt. Flashlights swept over backyards, lanes, and streets. Calls went out to families around Wheaton. Police were dispatched, and soon the tranquil suburban area was filled with the roar of sirens and the flash of headlights.

The word traveled fast, first via phone calls, then through radio and television. By the following morning, Wheaton was a community in shock. Schools swarmed with murmurs. Parents hugged their children closer. The notion that two sisters may go into a shopping complex and never return instilled horror into every home.

Reporters mobbed the neighborhood. Cameras caught the anxious expressions of neighbors, the grim resolve of police officers, and the sad eyes of John and Mary Lyon as they pleaded for their daughters' release.

At a news conference, John Lyon, a well-known local radio personality, tried to preserve his calm.

> "Please," he begged, his voice shaking but adamant, "if anyone has seen my girls, if anyone knows anything—come forward. We simply want them home."

The cry boomed throughout the radio, impressing itself on a national audience. But no responses came.

Instead, questions grew. How did two youngsters disappear in broad daylight, surrounded by hundreds of people? Who was the guy with the tape recorder? Why had no one detected things sooner?

Detectives labored into the night, seeking clues that slipped through their fingers. Witness statements contradicted one another. Timelines overlapped, leaving detectives with a jigsaw lacking its most critical elements.

The worry spread like a stain. Parents who earlier allowed youngsters to wander freely now confined them inside. Streets that had previously echoed with laughter seemed eerily empty. Wheaton Plaza, once a vibrant center, conveyed an aura of dread.

One neighbor summed it up perfectly with a shudder:

> "We thought things like this happened in big cities, not here. Not to them. Not in Wheaton."

As the initial days went into weeks, the Lyons' house became a symbol of loss and uncertainty. Each tap at the door offered a flash of hope—only to be shattered by yet another false lead.

What started as a family's misery has become a national mystery. And as the days drew on, the unanswered questions got darker: Were the girls still alive? Had someone been observing them long before that spring afternoon? And if so, why had no one noticed the threat coming?

The disappearance of Sheila and Katherine Lyon was no longer merely a case. It was a wound that would never completely heal—a wound that raised a terrible reality.

Evil has made its way to Wheaton, Maryland. And it was only just starting to unveil itself.

CHAPTER 1

Wheaton Plaza

Wheaton Plaza in March 1975 was a tribute to suburban living. Stretching over acres of stores, colorful displays, and packed pathways, it symbolized both freedom and familiarity to local families. To Sheila and Katherine Lyon, it was the location where they could flip through records at the music shop, taste-test samples at the sweets counter, and stare at the beautiful window displays as if each establishment promised a new adventure.

On that particular spring afternoon, the plaza was alive with its regular chorus: the squeak of children's shoes on polished floors, the distant clatter of plates in the food court, and the incessant murmur of voices mixing into one steady cacophony. A combination of perfume, fried food, and fresh pretzels hovered in the air.

The sisters were spotted weaving through the throng, Katherine skipping ahead at parts, Sheila stopping to look at exhibits. Witnesses remembered their light-colored coats and the little pocketbook that one of them carried, swaying back and forth as they went.

Mrs. Pauline Johnson, a neighborhood shopper, would later tell investigators:

> "They were standing by the Orange Bowl stand, sipping their drinks. I recall because they were laughing — it was the type of laugh that made you look. Happy, careless. Just two young girls."

Another witness, an older kid who worked at a neighboring record shop, remembered:

> "They came in around three, I think. The younger one was pointing at a poster of David Cassidy. They weren't in any hurry."

It seemed ordinary at the moment. Two sisters, enjoying a Saturday at the mall. But as history would reveal, these casual glimpses were the final bits of their regular lives—the last time anybody in the public could declare for certain that they saw Sheila and Katherine Lyon.

Even in such a crowded, public setting, a predator may hide. And at Wheaton Plaza that day, numerous individuals would later say they spotted a guy studying the girls too closely.

As detectives gathered together statements, discrepancies started to arise. Some reported the girls were last seen in the record shop. Others said they observed them exiting the plaza, headed toward the street. A few noticed a guy with a tape recorder approaching youngsters and requesting them to talk into his microphone.

Mrs. Johnson, when re-interviewed, added more uneasily:

> "Now that I think of it... there was a man nearby. Tall, slender. He continued toying with something in his hands, like a small recorder. I blew it off at the time, but... he was near. Too close."

Another shopper described him differently:

> "He looked scruffy, maybe in his twenties or thirties. He was asking them questions – like what they liked to eat, or where they lived. I thought that was unusual, but back then... people didn't respond the way we would now."

Police observed how descriptions differed. Was it one individual or several? Was the tape recorder detail a distraction or the key?

Detective Joseph Sargent would later recount his frustration:

> "It was like trying to hold water in your hands. Every witness offered you something, but nothing lined up. And every hour that passed... those girls were drifting farther away."

The unpleasant fact was that the plaza, packed as it was, had afforded a predator anonymity. Shoppers were focused on deals, families on errands, and youth on music and movies. In all that bustle and action, two small girls might hide—unseen until it was too late.

A friend of the Lyon family, who had gone to the square the same day, recalls the unsettling sense that hindsight etched into memory:

> "I saw them from a distance. Just for a time. They were walking for the exit. And I swear there was someone behind them - someone observing. I didn't think much of it then. God, if I had just stopped them..."

By dark, those lingering shadows became the case's first disturbing riddle. Was it the tape recorder man? Another stranger among the crowd? Or had the females just slipped away, unseen?

The plaza, once a haven of childish delight, had morphed in memory into a stage where innocence was eaten whole.

And somewhere in that throng, it seemed, the hunter had already selected his target.

CHAPTER 2

Vanishing Point

By late afternoon on March 25, 1975, the lively buzz of Wheaton Plaza continued as if nothing remarkable were occurring. Shoppers poured in and out of establishments, unknowing that somewhere in those packed halls, two sisters had slipped out of sight—and into history.

The last firm chronology placed Sheila and Katherine at the Orange Bowl snack counter at about 2:30 p.m., drinking their beverages and conversing like any other day. A short time later, a buddy reported seeing them near the record shop. By 3:00 p.m., another friend said they were moving for the exit, presumably to make the trek home.

And then—nothing.

Between those times, the route terminated. No one noticed them cross the street. No one remembers them waiting for the bus. No neighbor observed them on the regular trip back to their home. They simply disappeared, like the throng itself had closed around them.

Detectives subsequently recreated those last minutes with great care. Was it at the entryway of the mall when they disappeared? Somewhere between a store and the parking lot? Or had someone taken them aside, captivated by curiosity, before they even reached the street?

The mystery increased with every interview. Witnesses contradicted one another. Times blurred. Some swore the girls departed alone; others claimed they spotted a guy pursuing them. The truth seemed increasingly brittle the closer investigators drew in, as if memory itself was splintering beneath the weight of what had transpired.

> "It was broad daylight," one investigator would later comment. "You expect danger in the shadows, in empty streets. But at a mall, crowded with people? That's what made it so terrifying."

Somewhere in that small space, the usual morphed into the unfathomable.

At the Lyon residence, the clock crept beyond four o'clock. Sheila and Katherine were anticipated back by then. Their mother, Mary, peeked out the window numerous times, eager to see the familiar image of the girls going up the street.

By 4:15, the house was strained.

> "They're just late," Mary remarked loudly, almost to herself. "Maybe they stopped at the record store again."

Their father, John Lyon, a local radio broadcaster, attempted to soothe her, but concern was quickly seeping into his voice.

> "They know they're supposed to be home by now. But you're correct. They'll come through the door any minute."

But the minutes extended, and no footsteps approached.

By 5:00, Mary contacted a neighbor.

> "Have you seen the girls? They should have been home over an hour ago."

The neighbor hadn't. Panic started to thread her sentences. She contacted Wheaton Plaza, asking whether anybody had seen two young girls in light jackets. Nothing.

When John drove the short distance to the plaza personally, he explored the pathways, glanced into the food court, and inspected every area where youngsters could loiter. The mall, once loud and lively, now seemed cavernous and uninterested. The females were not there.

By dusk, the first calls to police were made. Officers replied kindly at first, advising the parents that occasionally toddlers "lose track of time." But Mary's voice pierced through the serenity.

> "Not Sheila and Katherine. Not both of them together. Something's wrong."

At 7:00, search activities started in earnest. Friends fanned over the area, yelling the girls' names into the twilight. Flashlights swept over backyards and alleyways. The once-ordinary Tuesday night became the start of a nightmare.

Detective Sergeant subsequently recounted the bleak turning point:

> "At first, you tell yourself — they're at a friend's, they'll walk in any minute. But then the hours drag on. And you know time is draining away. Every minute is a door closing."

By midnight, optimism that the girls had just been delayed had faded. The Lyons' house overflowed with friends, neighbors, and uniformed cops. The phone rang incessantly. The street outside swarmed with spotlights and frantic footsteps.

Mary sat in the kitchen, cradling a cup of untouched tea.

> "It's dark," she mumbled. "They're out there in the dark."

And at that instant, the community understood: something inconceivable had occurred. The innocence of Wheaton had broken. Two sisters were gone, devoured between one sighting and the next. And no one knew where to begin to locate them.

CHAPTER 3

The Hunt Begins

The Lyon house had turned overnight from a haven of love and laughter into a nerve center of feverish activity. The living room table, previously crowded with schoolbooks and schoolwork, was now covered with notepads, cellphones, and hurriedly written lists of people to contact.

Mary Lyon sat in her chair, hands quivering as she folded leaflet after poster. The grainy black-and-white images of her girls gazed back at her—grins frozen, eyes wide, naive. She squeezed each page flat as if the act itself may somehow keep them near.

John Lyon, typically composed behind his radio microphone, found himself stammering during interviews. On local stations and subsequently national broadcasts, his voice broke beneath the weight of sadness.

"Please, if you've seen Sheila and Katherine... if you know anything... bring them back. Our daughters are kids. They don't run away. They're out there, and we need them home."

Neighbors rallied instantly. Kitchens converted into improvised print shops. Church members came to glue leaflets to telephone poles, stick them to store windows, and shove them into strangers' hands. Children at nearby schools were instructed to keep alert and to report their parents if they had seen or heard anything suspicious.

One neighbor recalls those long nights vividly: "Mary was hollow-eyed, just moving on instinct. She wouldn't eat. I won't sleep. She just kept asking us, 'Have you checked this street? What about that corner?' You couldn't say no. You just went."

The Lyons' cries became the lifeblood of the quest. Their pain was genuine and unfiltered, and it stretched far beyond Wheaton. By the second day, their narrative was moving faster than they could imagine.

Section 2: Police and Public Pressure

Montgomery County police, unprepared for a disappearance of this size, suddenly found themselves in the heart of a maelstrom. Dozens of cops scoured through woodlands, streams, and abandoned houses.

Helicopters flew above, their searchlights slashing across fields as if to expose the shadows where answers lay.

Detective Sargent recounted the intense feeling of urgency: "You could feel the whole town breathing down your neck. Every face you saw on the street seemed to say, "Why haven't you discovered them yet?"

The case rapidly soared into headlines. "Two Sisters Vanish in Wheaton," blared the headlines. Local television stations provided nightly reports, cameras flashing as cops hauled boxes of tips into the station. The news moved to the national wires, quickly appearing in publications throughout the country.

The Lyon family stood before microphones, their cheeks blanched beneath the glaring lights. John's voice was hoarse, his words cracking.

"We will not stop searching. If you know anything at all—even the least information—please, please come forward."

Behind the scenes, police lines were overloaded with calls. Some recommendations were earnest; others bordered on hysterical. Dozens of reported sightings flooded in from around Maryland and beyond, each leading to hasty checks and obvious dead ends.

A Wheaton local recalls the anxiety clearly: "Parents didn't let their kids out of sight, not even to walk down the block. The entire town was on edge. If two small children could vanish from Wheaton Plaza, it could happen anywhere."

Reporters pressured the cops every day. Cameras recorded heated conversations as the media requested updates.

"Detective, do you have any suspects?"

"Are you closer to finding the girls?"

The responses were deliberate and calculated, but the strain showed.

"We're following every lead," Sergeant continued. "Every available resource is in this case."

But the unsaid fact lingered: with every hour that went, the odds of finding Sheila and Katherine alive appeared to lessen.

The media frenzy, the countless fliers, the frantic appeals—everything fused into a single, unsettling question: how could two sisters disappear in broad daylight, and how could no one see where they went?

As the spotlight became brighter, the Lyons' pain increased, and the police readied themselves for a search that was swiftly spiraling beyond anyone's control.

The chase had started—and it would alter Wheaton forever.

CHAPTER 4

Suspicions and Leads

In the initial frantic days of the inquiry, one name started to reverberate through police reports and neighborhood conversations: the guy with the tape recorder.

Witnesses described him as scrawny and scruffy, with a peculiar propensity for approaching youngsters at Wheaton Plaza. He carried a little recorder, asking them to talk into the microphone about what cuisines they loved, what programs they watched, and where they lived. At first sight, it would have appeared innocuous—odd at worst. But in the aftermath of Sheila and Katherine's disappearance, everything seemed ominous.

Detectives sat opposite from a teenage witness who had seen the guy that day.

> "He walked right up to me," the child recounted, squirming in his chair. "Said he was doing some kind of

survey. Wanted me to speak my favorite ice cream flavor into the recorder."

"Did he say who he worked for?" the investigator pushed.

"No. That's the thing. He simply continued smiling. I didn't like it, so I went away."

Another little girl remembered how the man's queries got unnerving.

> "He asked if I lived nearby. I didn't answer. He laughed, like it was a game."

"What did he look like?" the officer inquired softly.

She hesitated. "Tall. Stringy hair. His eyes... I don't know. Something about his eyes."

Parents shuddered as word spread. In whispered conversations at grocery stores and church basements, his figure loomed larger.

Mary Lyon, her voice breaking, asked detectives directly:

> "Could this man have taken them? My girls would've trusted someone who smiled at them. Did he—"

"We're investigating every possibility," the detective interrupted, though his tone betrayed unease.

Posters soon bore not only the faces of Sheila and Katherine but also sketches of the Tape Recorder Man, based on the fragments of memory children had provided. He became both a lead and a symbol of dread—the stranger every parent now feared might be lurking just beyond their sight.

As the weeks stretched on, the case took darker turns. Tips poured in—hundreds, then thousands—and detectives chased them with growing desperation.

One man confessed outright, claiming he had lured the girls away. Detectives leaned forward, notebooks ready.

> "Where did you see them? What did you do?"

The man spun a tale that unraveled within hours. He hadn't even been in Maryland on March 25.

Another lead came from a woman certain she'd spotted the sisters boarding a bus hours after their disappearance. Investigators tracked the driver, interviewed passengers, and compared times. Nothing matched.

Detective Sergeant recalled the frustration years later:

> "Every false lead chewed up hours we didn't have. You'd run it down, thinking — this could be it — only to hit another wall. And meanwhile, the real trail was going cold."

Even the Tape Recorder Man became a maze. Multiple individuals fit the vague description. Some were tracked down and interviewed, their recorders harmless, their intentions odd but not criminal. Others vanished back into anonymity, never identified.

In one heated late-night meeting, John Lyon confronted detectives.

> "So many leads — and none of them bring my daughters home. How do you explain that?"

The detective hesitated, exhaustion clear on his face. "Mr. Lyon, we're working day and night. But these trails... they twist and disappear. We're not giving up."

For the community, each false report stoked both hope and heartbreak. Flyers spread farther, sightings were phoned in from across state lines, but none brought the sisters closer.

By summer, frustration settled over Wheaton like a heavy fog. The girls were still missing, the leads collapsing one by one, and every whisper of the Tape

Recorder Man lingered like a ghost story—never proven, never forgotten.

The case was no longer just about two missing sisters. It was about the terrifying reality that in a world full of witnesses, truth could still hide in plain sight.

CHAPTER 5

The Case Grows Cold

In the beginning, the Lyons had lived by the phone. Every ring jolted Mary and John upright—a tip, a sighting, a hope. But as months turned into years, the calls slowed, then nearly stopped.

Detectives who had once pounded pavement daily found themselves relegated to thin case updates and aging file folders. The leads were gone. Witnesses moved. Memories blurred.

Detective Clark admitted years later:

> "It never leaves you. Every time you open a missing persons report, you remember the ones you couldn't bring home. The Lyon girls... they were always there in the back of my mind."

At the family's dinner table, silence filled the spaces where laughter used to be. Sheila and Katherine's chairs stayed tucked away, but their absence was louder than words.

Mary often caught herself setting out too many plates. She would stop, stare at the extra dish, and quietly return it to the cabinet.

One evening, John broke the silence:

> "Do you think people will remember, Mary? Years from now?"

She looked at him, her voice trembling. "I don't care if the world forgets. I just don't want us to."

Birthdays passed without candles. Christmases came and went with unopened stockings. The Lyons held onto hope, but it was a brittle hope, fragile and cracking under time's weight.

For detectives, anniversaries were reminders of failure. A new batch of rookies might pull the case file, read the notes, and ask questions—but no one could move it forward. The unanswered questions loomed larger with every year of silence.

As time stretched into decades, the case took on a life of its own. In Wheaton, theories became part of local lore. Some swore the girls had been taken by a traveling predator. Others whispered about organized crime, trafficking rings, and even occult rumors that made their way into late-night radio chatter.

At a neighborhood gathering, the conversations were hushed but unrelenting.

> "I heard they were seen in Pennsylvania," one neighbor muttered.

Another shook his head. "No. My cousin's sure she read about them in California years later."

"And yet here we are," an older man said bitterly, "no bodies, no answers."

Theories swirled faster than facts. The Tape Recorder Man, the mall itself, and even family acquaintances came under suspicion in whispered conversations. The silence left a vacuum, and rumors rushed to fill it.

In a rare interview years later, John Lyon reflected on the enduring mystery:

> "Not knowing... that's the cruelest part. If they were gone, if we had something — anything — to hold onto, maybe we could have grieved properly. But every day is a question mark."

Reporters who had once crowded the Lyons' front lawn moved on to other stories, but anniversaries always brought them back. Cameras would flash, and microphones would be shoved forward.

> "Mr. Lyon, do you still believe your daughters are alive?"

John's jaw tightened. "I believe they deserve to be found. Alive or not—they deserve that much."

The unanswered questions weighed heavily on the community too. Parents told their children the story like a warning: Don't talk to strangers. Don't wander alone. Remember the Lyon sisters.

But in every retelling, one truth remained the same—no one knew what had happened.

Why had the trail gone cold so quickly?

Who was the Tape Recorder Man, really?

Had the girls trusted someone they shouldn't have, or had they been snatched in a moment of fate no one could prevent?

The questions echoed through Wheaton's streets for decades, long after the flyers had yellowed and the headlines had faded.

The Lyons carried them in silence. The detectives carried them in shame. The community carried them in whispers.

And the answers—if they ever existed—stayed buried in the shadows of March 25, 1975.

CHAPTER 6

A Break in Time

By the early 2000s, the Lyon sisters' case had become a shadow in Montgomery County. A cold case, stored away in dusty files heaped shoulder-high in the police archives.

But as forensic technology evolved, so did the promise of second chances. DNA databases expanded. Interview tactics refined. Old evidence, previously thought worthless, received fresh weight.

Detective Mark Janney removed one of the heavy folders from the shelf in 2013. He scattered images, hand-scrawled notes, and transcripts on a table. Decades-old handwriting faded by fluorescent light.

"Look at this," Janney replied, referring to an early report. "We had a suspect who gave a statement at the time. Lloyd Welch. Just a wanderer. But his name crops up more than once."

His companion drew closer. "Back then, he was just a kid, right? Seventeen?"

"Seventeen," Janney affirmed. "But listen—he inserted himself into the case. Lied about what he witnessed. Then it disappeared."

The room became quiet. For investigators who had borne the weight of failure, the thought that anything had been lying in plain sight all these years was astonishing.

One cop whispered what they all felt:

> "What if we had him all along?"

The process of reviewing the evidence was meticulous. Witness testimony was reread, cross-referenced, and digitized. Old tips, earlier ignored, were recovered from manila envelopes.

"Technology may not solve everything," Janney told his staff during a late-night assessment, "but perspective will. We're not the same investigators they were in 1975. We know better. We perceive differently."

The further they probed, the more they discovered that Welch's tale—the one put aside as inconsequential—didn't add up.

Lloyd Lee Welch had been little more than a blip in the first probe. An adolescent fugitive with a history of falsehoods, jailed for little offenses, traveling from place to town.

But in 2014, when his name appeared again, detectives realized he was no longer simply a small footnote. His record had enlarged—and it was terrifying. Multiple convictions. A documented pattern of predatory conduct.

Detective Janney sat in the gloomy interview room, a file open before him. Across the table, an investigator from Virginia glanced through mugshots of Welch from the '80s and '90s.

"Look at his eyes," she muttered. "He's aged, but the pattern hasn't changed. He targets youngsters. Always has."

Janney tapped the original transcript from 1975.

> "He said he saw two girls being forced into a car at Wheaton Plaza. But the information he gave? Impossible. They didn't fit the setting. He was lying."

"Why lie," his companion queried, "unless he was covering his own involvement?"

The question hovered in the air like a blade.

As they investigated Welch's background, a worse picture emerged. He has links to Bedford County, Virginia. Family members there murmured of alarming conduct, rumors that had never reached Maryland police in 1975.

Agents proceeded south to delve further.

One evening, gathered in a creaky farmhouse, they questioned an old cousin.

> "Did Lloyd ever talk about Maryland?"

The guy shuffled uncomfortably. "He said things... things I didn't want to hear. About those females. I convinced myself he was simply boasting, making it up. But maybe..."

The words drifted off, laden with sadness.

Back in Montgomery County, Janney addressed his troops.

> "For nearly forty years, we've chased shadows. This isn't a shadow. It's flesh and blood. Lloyd Welch has been right there, sliding between the cracks."

Another investigator closed the case with finality.

> "Then it's time we stop treating him as a footnote."

By the time authorities formally labeled Welch as a suspect, the investigation had moved from frigid quiet to eager pursuit. The halls of the precinct hummed with the type of excitement many feared they'd never experience on the Lyon case again.

Journalists got wind, and murmurs turned into headlines: "New Suspect in 1975 Lyon Sisters Case."

For the Lyon family, it was a stomach hit—not relief, not closure, but a scary new chapter.

Mary Lyon, her voice tired but calm, talked to a reporter on her porch.

> "For years, we prayed for answers. Now, if this guy knows anything — if he's the reason my girls never returned home — I need the truth. I don't care how long it takes."

And so, after decades of stillness, the past fought its way back into the present.

The name Lloyd Welch was no longer an afterthought. It was a storm cloud, black and brooding, ready to burst wide open.

The detectives knew: this was no ordinary lead. This was the thread that, if plucked, may unravel everything buried since March 25, 1975.

CHAPTER 7

Into Darkness

Lloyd Lee read like a caution sign missed too many times. Born into instability, nurtured in fragmented houses, he bore wounds of neglect and wrath long before his name ever appeared in a police report.

Teachers recalled a child who floated around classes without attention. He lied easily, stole from peers, and lashed out when exposed. Neighbors described him as "a shadow at the edge of things," the boy who loitered too long, looking at children on playgrounds.

By his adolescent years, Welch had already gained a record. Petty stealing. Breaking into residences. But behind those acts flowed a deeper stream—a history of unsettling conduct with youngsters, talked about but seldom tackled openly.

Detective Mark Janney subsequently remarked in an interview:

> "It wasn't just what he did. It was the way he traveled from place to place, leaving harm behind him. He was constantly floating, always concealing. He didn't want roots – he wanted shadows."

Psychologists who subsequently analyzed Welch's record characterized him as a manipulator, someone who sought control in the most vulnerable. He was opportunistic, volatile, and extremely deceitful.

A parole officer once wrote in a report from the early 1980s:

> "Mr. Welch exhibits a disturbing lack of remorse. He denies, then concedes, then denies again. His actions implies he is not merely a criminal but a predator."

As the years proceeded, his arrests grew—drug charges, sexual assault claims, and violent outbursts. He slipped in and out of prison, spending time, then reemerging with the same habits.

Investigators looking back saw the image of a guy society failed to stop. Each ignored crime, each silent discharge, created the opportunity for something worse.

And in the setting of the Lyon sisters, that potential evolved into a nightmare.

When investigators reviewed the Lyon case and put Welch under examination, the pieces started to fit together with chilling clarity.

It began with his falsehoods. In 1975, he had claimed to observe the girls being pushed into a vehicle near Wheaton Plaza. But when police probed him decades later, his tale evolved. He confessed more. Then denied again. Then confessed worse.

Sitting across from investigators in a sterile jail room, Welch fidgeted, eyes flashing, voice low.

> "I was there," he muttered. "I saw them. I… I helped."

The detectives leaned forward.

> "Help how, Lloyd?"

His comments came out broken and contradictory but unmistakably damning. He talked of transferring the girls, of elder relatives engaged, of things that investigators found hard to put into official reports without flinching.

"Did you touch them?" one cop inquired.

Welch stared down at his hands.

> "I don't want to say it. You'll despise me. Everybody will despise me."

> "We need the truth," the detective said, steady but cold.

The room filled with a stillness so deep it seemed to suffocate the air. Finally, Welch muttered:

> "They didn't make it. None of them ever make it."

His explanations were disjointed and inconsistent in substance but consistent in implication: he had played a direct role in the disappearance and presumably the killings of Sheila and Katherine Lyon.

Investigators then proceeded to Bedford County, Virginia, where Welch's family resided. There, testimony heightened the misery. Family members described being instructed to burn bags of clothes. Others recalled Welch coming to one hot spring in 1975, frightened, bearing tales that made no sense.

One relative admitted in a recorded interview:

> "He came back talking about those girls. He said... he claimed they were gone. I didn't believe him. I figured that was simply Lloyd boasting again. But now? God help me, maybe it wasn't."

These testimonies, when layered against Welch's own confessions, made a terrifying mosaic. Not every piece fit precisely, but the overall image was obvious.

Detective Janney subsequently detailed the moment he knew Welch wasn't simply another suspect.

> "It hit me like a gut punch. For years, we assumed he was a liar, a wannabe witness. But the truth? He was worse than we could have imagined."

The probe reached a bleak crescendo when Welch, pushed further, divulged facts investigators had never published publicly. He mentioned areas in Virginia. He alluded to a fire. He remembered, with uncanny clarity, the outfit the sisters had worn that day.

One investigator turned to another when the interview finished.

> "This is it. He's not bluffing anymore. He knows too much."

Yet Welch's remarks were never linear. He evaded, refuted, and pushed responsibility onto others. It was as if he took a strange joy in dangling fragments of the truth without ever giving investigators the entire picture.

And thus, the Lyon case went from a compelling mystery into a sad reality: the sisters had very probably met encounters with Welch.

But what precisely transpired in those closing hours—and who else may have been involved—remained veiled in shadows.

As prosecutors studied the evidence, one thing became clear: Welch's history and present combined into something horrible. He was no longer merely "a troubled man." He was the epitome of the gloom that has lingered over Wheaton since 1975.

The terrifying fact was this: the Lyon sisters had undoubtedly fallen into his clutches, and once they did, there was no escape.

CHAPTER 8

Justice on Trial

The courthouse in Bedford County, Virginia, stood as a somber stage for a trial that had been forty years in the making. The Lyon family sat in the front rows, their features lined by decades of waiting. Investigators who had carried the case across generations filed onto the seats behind them. The air was oppressive, as if everyone inside understood they were not merely hearing a case—they were bearing the weight of history.

Lloyd Lee Welch trudged into the courtroom, thinner now, his prison uniform falling slack on his body. Shackles clinked as deputies took him to the defense table. For many, it was the first time they had seen the guy who had plagued their town for so long.

The prosecution started with a short, cutting line:

> "For more than forty years, the Lyon family has waited for answers. Today, you shall hear the truth."

The jurors leaned forward as prosecutors laid forth their case. They started not with guesswork but with Welch's own words—the contradicting interviews he had given over the years. Audio recordings played in the courtroom, his voice swinging from arrogant to evasive, then to chillingly matter-of-fact.

"I was there," Welch admits in one tape, his tone lifeless. "I helped."

The words resonated across the room like a razor dragged over stone.

Prosecutors crafted their argument block by block. Testimonies from family in Virginia detailed how Welch came home in 1975 carrying suitcases, demanding they be burnt. Others told of hushed admissions and frightening statements made in the quiet corners of family gatherings.

One relative took the stand, his voice shaking.

> "He told me... he assured me they weren't coming back. That the girls were gone. I didn't believe him then. God forgive me, I didn't believe him."

The defense reacted, painting Welch as a liar, a vagabond who desired attention, and a guy whose changing statements could not be believed. They pounded the contradictions, the holes in the evidence, and the absence of tangible remnants.

"Ladies and gentlemen," the defense counsel stated, "this is not justice. This is desperation. You cannot condemn a guy based on shadows and rumors."

But the prosecution focused on the unsettling consistency behind Welch's discrepancies. Each time he talked, he divulged a sliver more than before—facts that only someone involved could have known.

Detective Mark Janney testified, his voice calm yet weighted with years of sorrow.

> "We chased this case for decades. Every wrong lead, every dead end, it all led back to this guy. He was never a witness. He was never a bystander. He was always part of the crime."

The courtroom got heated with every disclosure. Jurors squirmed uneasily as prosecutors sketched the picture: two young girls recruited, carried over state lines, and silenced forever.

And yet, as overwhelming as the evidence was, it was incomplete. No bodies. No definite timeframe. Just words, testimony, and the deep suspicion that Welch was not alone in what transpired.

Still, the picture of Lloyd Welch—not as a harmless vagrant but as the evil monster hiding behind the Lyon sisters' abduction—hovered in the room, unavoidable.

When the jury filed back into the courtroom, the hush was total. The Lyon family sat hand in hand, preparing themselves for words they had longed to hear for over half a century.

The foreman rose, voice calm.

> "We, the jury, find the defendant, Lloyd Lee Welch... guilty."

Gasps rippled around the room. Some cried softly. Others just lowered their heads, letting the weight of the occasion sink in.

The judge gave the sentence: Welch would spend the rest of his life in jail, never to walk free again.

For the Lyon family, it was both everything and not enough. After the hearing, John Lyon spoke gently to reporters.

> "This is justice, yes. But it isn't closure. We still don't know where our daughters are. We still don't get them back."

His wife, Mary, said with tears in her eyes:

> "We waited forty years for this. We'll wait as long as it takes for the rest."

In the gallery, Detective Janney sat with his hands clutched firmly, looking at Welch. Later, he confessed to a colleague:

> "We got him. But it doesn't feel like triumph. It seems like a shadow that will never entirely lift."

For all the passion in the courtroom, a disturbing void remained. No one could state with confidence what had transpired in those closing hours of 1975. No one could bring the sisters home.

As the courtroom emptied, a question remained like a ghost in the air:

Has justice actually been served? Or had the trial simply provided a partial truth, keeping the complete narrative buried forever?

CHAPTER 9

The Echoes Remain

The Lyon residence in Kensington, Maryland, was never the same after March 1975. Even decades later, it retained a quiet that seemed to vibrate through the walls. Photographs of Sheila and Katherine remained displayed on mantels and tucked into books, not as decorations but as tributes.

For John and Mary Lyon, every holiday came with an empty chair. Every birthday was both a recollection and a hurt. Yet, despite unspeakable grief, they held themselves with calm dignity.

John Lyon kept working in radio broadcasting. His recognizable voice touched homes throughout the area even as his own heart bore silent grief. Off the radio, he became an advocate for missing children, adamant that his daughters' names would not fade from memory.

Mary Lyon committed herself to community service, her perseverance valued by neighbors. She once told a reporter, her voice quiet yet resolute:

> "You won't stop being their mother. You simply carry them differently."

The boys, Jay and Joe, grew into adults under the long shadow of their sisters' absence. They seldom talked publicly about the case, but those who knew them said they bore an unseen weight, each milestone in life weighed against the death of their sisters.

The Lyons commemorated anniversaries privately, gathering in silent thought rather than public commemoration. They lit candles, went through family photos, and prayed. For them, recollection was both a responsibility and a wound they could not seal.

Neighbors, too, never forgot. Wheaton was no longer merely the suburb where people shopped, worked, and raised children. It became linked with a crime that robbed innocence from the whole town. Parents who had earlier allowed their children to wander free now held them near, constantly remembering the Lyons' tragedy.

One lifelong resident commented years later:

> "That day changed all of us. It wasn't simply their family that lost anything. We all did."

The anguish endured, engraved into time. Even as decades passed, Sheila and Katherine remained fifteen and twelve—locked in the spring of 1975, never permitted to grow up in the world's sight.

The trial of Lloyd Welch provided responsibility, but it did not deliver all the answers. In fact, it intensified some questions. Investigators cobbled together aspects of Welch's story: the transfer of the girls to Virginia, the participation of relatives, and the fires that may have destroyed evidence. Yet the tale was incomplete. Welch contradicted himself in every recounting, shifting responsibility, concealing information, and tormenting investigators with half-truths.

Detective Mark Janney acknowledged in one interview:

> "We know he was involved. We know he lied. But we still don't know the complete story. We don't know where they are."

That reality— or rather, that lack of truth—is what continues to torment Wheaton. No bodies were ever found. No exact chronology was ever determined. No one can tell with confidence what transpired in those dying hours.

Even still, murmurs abound about others who may have been involved. Welch alluded to accomplices, family members who helped bury evidence. Some were explored. Some testified. Yet no one else was ever charged.

One former detective stated it bluntly:

> "We may have only scratched the surface. The remainder of the narrative might yet be buried in Virginia soil."

The Lyon sisters' case left behind a trail of frightening "what ifs."

What if cops had moved more rapidly in 1975?

What if early suspicions had been pursued harder?

What if someone, somewhere, still possesses the missing piece of truth?

For the Lyon family, such questions stung deeply. Justice had arrived, but closure had not. In interviews following Welch's conviction, John Lyon consistently went back to one plea:

> "If there is anyone left who knows anything, tell us. Give us our girls back, if only in truth."

The frightening speculation lingers. Could remains still be concealed in the forests of Bedford County? Did others take secrets to their graves? And perhaps most terrifying of all—is it conceivable that the complete tale of what happened to Sheila and Katherine may never be known? Wheaton Plaza, recently refurbished and renamed Westfield Wheaton, still bustles with consumers. Families visit the same grounds where the sisters were last seen. Few detect the ghosts under their footsteps. But for those who remember, the echoes persist.

A shopkeeper, questioned about the case decades later, shrugged his head.

> "People move on, the mall changes, but for some of us, it's always 1975 here. Always those girls."

The Lyon sisters' tale is not only a tragedy stuck in time. It is a mirror held up to a nation's weakness—a reminder of how fast innocence can be snatched, how long justice can take, and how delicate closure truly is.

For every reader, every neighbor, and every detective who touched this case, one thing remains unavoidable: the tale is not complete. And so the question hangs, as weighty and frightening as ever:

Are there still mysteries hidden in the shadows of Wheaton?

EPILOGUE

Ghosts of Wheaton Plaza

Nearly half a century later, the disappearance of Sheila and Katherine Lyon remains a scar that never entirely healed. Lloyd Welch's conviction delivered responsibility, but it did not give a whole truth. No bodies were ever found. No one knows exactly what occurred in those last hours after the girls were enticed from Wheaton Plaza.

Welch's admissions were replete with discrepancies—changing timings, half-named accomplices, and purposeful omissions.Investigators suspect others may have had a part, but those leads were too broken to obtain charges. Some prospective witnesses are gone now, their secrets buried with them. Others may still live with information they have never shared.

Theories persist. Were the girls transferred to Virginia and silenced there? Were their bodies incinerated in the flames Welch alluded to? Or may shards of truth still lie hidden in the forests and hills where searchers previously dug?

Detectives acknowledge that these questions may never be addressed. What remains is not clarity but silence—the most terrifying legacy of all.

And so, the ghosts of Wheaton Plaza persist, floating in the gaps where truth stops and interpretation starts.

The Lyon sisters' case altered America. It undermined the notion that suburban life was impenetrable, forcing families to face an unpleasant truth: innocence could be gone in an instant.

After 1975, parents kept their children closer. Communities reexamined safety. Law enforcement started treating missing kid investigations with a new intensity, realizing how fast precious hours may slip away. Advocacy organizations for missing and exploited children developed from tragedies like these, spurred by the urge to prevent such atrocities from occurring again.

For the Lyons, survival meant dignity in mourning. For Wheaton, survival meant bearing memory as both a burden and a warning. And for the country, survival required never forgetting that evil may walk softly among the everyday.

Today, the retail complex is bright and busy, rebuilt and refurbished, although underneath the shiny stores lurks a darker history. Those who know the tale feel it still—an intangible weight, a whisper of two girls who never came home.

The tale of Sheila and Katherine Lyon is not merely history. It is a mirror held to every parent, every town, and every culture that fancies itself safe.

The message is obvious, persistent, and unresolved: justice may punish, but it cannot repair. And sometimes, the truth stays eternally just out of grasp.

CLOSING SECTION

Lessons from the Shadows

Key Lessons Learned

The disappearance of Sheila and Katherine Lyon was not just a tragedy but also a turning point in how America treated missing children situations. From this scenario, numerous lessons emerge:

Justice is frequently partial. Convictions may provide responsibility, but they seldom give comprehensive answers. The Lyon case reminds us that courts deal in evidence, not in closure, and the most frightening realities might stay permanently buried.

Forensic science develops—but time is the enemy. When detectives examined the Lyon case decades later, DNA testing and behavioral research provided fresh options that were unavailable in 1975. Yet, vital chances had long ago passed away. The instance underscores that timely, evidence-driven actions are crucial—because after time passes, even the greatest technologies may not retrieve what was lost.

Community vigilance is important. In Wheaton, many spotted the girls. They observed strange people. But jumbled recollections and a lack of urgency delayed action. Today, the lesson is clear: what may seem like a simple remark might become the missing piece in solving a case.

The psychology of evil is misleading. Lloyd Welch seemed average, even forgettable, to many. Yet behind that veneer lay a lethal predator. This encourages us to reconsider assumptions of "the criminal"—many offenders depend on fitting in, not sticking out.

Modern Safety Strategies

The world of 1975 was different, yet danger has adapted, not gone. The lessons we apply today must be practical, evidence-based, and tailored to a digital age:

Physical safety: Encourage youngsters to develop "situational awareness"—observing who is around, where exits are, and when anything seems wrong. Self-defense is not simply physical but also about spotting danger before it escalates.

Digital safety: Predators no longer need malls to locate victims. Social media, gaming platforms, and chat applications have become hunting grounds. Families should freely address online conduct, create privacy limits, and cultivate healthy skepticism toward digital strangers.

Psychological awareness: Offenders typically influence trust by providing attention, gifts, or pity. Teaching both children and adults to understand manipulative methods—flattery, secrecy, urgency—is as crucial as physical caution.

Community prevention: The greatest defense is communal. Neighborhood monitors, parent networks, and digital safety organizations may generate shared accountability. One warning voice may be the difference between prevention and catastrophe.

Inside the Criminal Mind

Offenders like Lloyd Welch typically share worrisome psychological patterns:

Compulsion and escalation: Welch's background demonstrates how petty infractions and perverse thoughts frequently escalate uncontrolled into horrific crimes. Early intervention in such conduct is crucial.

Manipulation via normalcy: Predators are good at looking ordinary. Welch visited a mall in broad daylight, carrying a tape recorder, fitting into a throng where youngsters felt comfortable. This camouflage—disguising danger behind routine—is one of their most effective strategies.

Projection and deflection: Welch altered tales, blamed others, and twisted chronology. Offenders typically blend partial facts with falsehoods to dominate narratives. Understanding this strategy helps investigators—and the public—differentiate noise from reality.

Predatory persistence: Such people seldom cease without assistance. They thrive on opportunity and access. Communities must remember that predators are generally repeat offenders who develop their approaches over time.

Honoring the Victims

Too frequently, genuine crime reduces lives to footnotes in someone else's misery. Sheila and Katherine Lyon were more than victims—they were daughters, sisters, friends, and dreamers.

Sheila liked painting and singing, with a quick wit that lightened her family's days. Katherine was inquisitive, smart, and adventurous, typically the one suggesting new games or ideas. Together, they were inseparable—their closeness as sisters a daily thrill to anyone who knew them.

What was lost was not just two young lives but the futures they could have established—families of their own, jobs, friendships yet to be found. To celebrate them is to recall the joy in their house, the warmth of their presence, and the innocence they brought into Wheaton Plaza that spring day.

Extended Resources

For readers looking to take action, support families, or obtain aid, the following resources remain crucial. These organizations give not simply hotlines but full aid, from crisis intervention to long-term support:

U.S. National Center for Missing & Exploited Children (NCMEC): Website: https://www.missingkids.org

24/7 Hotline: 1-800-THE-LOST (1-800-843-5678)

Offers case assistance, preventative education, and family resources.

RAINN (Rape, Abuse & Incest National Network):

Website: https://www.rainn.org

Hotline: 1-800-656-HOPE (4673)

The biggest U.S. anti-sexual assault group, including therapy and legal assistance.

UK Missing People Charity: Website: https://www.missingpeople.org.uk Helpline: 116 000

Provides free, confidential help to missing persons and families throughout the UK.

Europol—Crimes Against Children (EU-wide):

Website: https://www.europol.europa.eu/crime-areas-and-trends/crimes-against-children

Coordinates international investigations and child protection measures.

International Centre for Missing & Exploited Children (ICMEC): Website: https://www.icmec.org

A worldwide organization advocating cross-border collaboration, legal change, and training.

These are not simply numbers and websites—they are lifelines, standing between danger and survival, quiet and justice.

Final Reflection

The Lyon sisters' tale is a disturbing reminder that human danger does not necessarily wear a mask of menacing. Sometimes it wanders in daytime, blending among crowds, hidden in plain sight.

But this narrative is not merely about dread. It is about resilience—the strength of families who bear terrible loss, of investigators who refuse to give up, and of communities that continue to carry memory as a warning.

We live in a world where innocence is vulnerable, but also where vigilance and understanding are great weapons. The ghosts of Wheaton Plaza encourage us not merely to remember Sheila and Katherine but to learn from their absence—to defend more fiercely, to question more aggressively, and to safeguard more fully.

The third lesson is simple but enduring: justice is not a destination but a quest. And the pursuit must never cease.

Printed in Dunstable, United Kingdom